RUSSIAN Parkinson's Law

A lecture by Yuri M Luzhkov, Mayor of Moscow, given at the International University

With a foreword by academician Yevgeny Velikhov

Illustrations by Alexey Merinov

Translated by David Kenworthy

Russian edition first published by VAGRIUS, 1999

Middlesex University
PRESS

First published in 2005 by Middlesex University Press

Copyright © Mayor of Moscow, Yuri M Luzhkov

Original Translation by Mr Ali Visaev

ISBN 1 904750 44 3

All rights reserved. No part of this publication may be reproduced, stored in any retrieval system or transmitted in any form or by any means, electronic, mechanical, photocopying, recording or otherwise, without the prior written permission of the copyright holder for which application should be addressed in the first instance to the publishers. No liability shall be attached to the author, the copyright holder or the publishers for loss or damage of any nature suffered as a result of reliance on the reproduction of any of the contents of this publication or any errors or omissions in its contents.

A CIP catalogue record for this book is available from
The British Library

Book design by Helen Taylor

Printed in the UK by Ashford Colour Press Ltd.

Middlesex University Press, Queensway, Enfield, Middlesex EN4 3SF
Tel: +44 (0)20 8411 5734: +44 (0)20 8880 4262
Fax: +44 (0)20 8411 5736

www.mupress.co.uk

Yuri Mikhailovich Luzhkov was born in 1936 and is a graduate of the Gubkin Moscow Oil and Gas Institute. He has held senior posts in different firms and organizations within the chemical industry. He has the title of Professor and was awarded the State Prize of the USSR.

Since 1987 he has occupied different positions within the executive of Moscow City Council: he has been first deputy Chairman of the Moscow City executive committee, Chairman of the city's department responsible for agri-business, Chairman of the executive committee of Moscow City Council and Deputy-Mayor. From June 1992 until June 1996 he carried out the responsibilities of the city's Mayor. Then in June 1996 and again in December 1999 and in December 2003 he was elected Mayor by popular vote of the city's population. He is a leading member of the political party United Russia.

With thanks to Mr Ali Visaev, Journalist, Mr Fazil Ibragimov and John C Florey without whose help this book would not have been possible.

Contents

i   Foreword by Yevgeny Velikhov
iii   Introduction by Ali Visaev

1   Russian Parkinson's Law

The Laws

11
The law of
Inevitable Distortions

17
The law of
Compulsory Cheating

23
The law of
'No, it's impossible'

27
The law of
Avos

31
The law of
Everything Now

37
The law of
By and Large

55   From the Mayor's Notepad

Foreword

I must acknowledge that it was I who persuaded Yuri Mikhailovich to publish this remarkable lecture, which is more in the nature of a brief philosophical and psychological essay, as a separate pamphlet. Not just because it made me laugh a lot, but because it made many things clear to me.

What the author is talking about is an age-old Russian problem. Our land is rich – but it is in a state of disorder, and there is no way of comprehending just why this should be. The scientific approach, which is so powerful in understanding nature, is of no help. In the Soviet period, Zhvanetskiy explained more than economic science. In the pre-Soviet period, too, Russians could be managed by common sense and apt words. And this is all the more true today.

It is welcome that one of our most experienced administrators, who has been through the gamut of management from running a chemical production facility to managing one of the most complex systems on our planet, the city of Moscow, has undertaken this task of analysis. But most remarkable is the fact that he is exploiting a new seam of popular wisdom, the wisdom of engineers, scientists, workers and officials.

Of course, at some point science will be able to put in its word. But when, and what sort of science will it be? Today so many decisions have to be taken in a climate of uncertainty and distorted, misinterpreted information, and the situation itself is changed by taking those decisions… I can tell you as a physicist that in such a climate the path of science is too long and difficult to provide instant solutions.

But we need to act now, and it's here that this brief guide to the new life with the old sins will come in very handy. I hope it will not only give you intellectual pleasure, but also be of practical use.

Yevgeny Velikhov

Introduction

When I was asked to write briefly about Mayor Luzhkov's professional and creative biography and the transformations in Moscow, I found myself thinking that they were the same thing – indeed, in recent years Yuri Mikhailovich has himself been creating the biography, or Modern History, of Moscow.

If the collapse of the Soviet Union was a tectonic event which changed the world order, Moscow was the epicentre of that elemental upheaval, and a man was needed who could saddle this upheaval, urge it on into the thick of the economic and political fray and emerge triumphant from the unequal fight. Today the world looks upon Moscow with hope, whatever remains to be improved. This in itself is enough to show that 'the Mayor has made his name in struggle'.

With the transformation of Moscow from the Soviet capital into one of the most beautiful capital cities of Europe, the Mayor has essentially shaped its Modern History. Along its whole revolutionary path from market stalls and wooden boxes on Tverskaya street, from the economic ruin of the transition period, to the international Auchan hypermarkets, the circumferential Metro, and a Moscow which today is one of the world's business and financial hubs, the city has been led by its Mayor.

The Soviet era produced much of human value and second-rate architecture. Moscow, while basically the capital of a Great Power, actually looked like a Third World city, and its reconstruction called for vast financial and economic resources on the basis of new relations between labour and capital.

While animated discussion was going on in the political world as to what path we should follow, Yuri Mikhailovich began to build his very own Moscow roads. Soon a 'ring road' that belonged to the era of Nikolai Vasilievich Gogol's Dead Souls was transformed into a modern motorway. A third circular road was built, allowing the traffic to move freely once again in Moscow. And so one of Russia's historical ills – Moscow's roads – was overcome. The building of the City business district symbolically and actually integrated Moscow into the ranks of world capitals. The creation of the Poklonnaya Gora monument gave a new meaning to civic heroism as a constant in the midst of changing political systems. Preservation and restoration of the entire historical and classical architectural heritage side by side with a rapidly evolving modern style is a combination that characterises Moscow today.

The architectural revival of Moscow was accompanied by a struggle between two opposite tendencies – a capitalism that was dubbed 'savage capitalism' in the West and the creation of a market economy by civilised methods.

The enormous service rendered by the Mayor was that he led the fight to forge a market economy by civilised methods, united able people around him, and threw open the doors to foreign investors.

The establishment of fully empowered companies, the involvement of international financial institutions in Moscow projects and participation in international investment forums created an atmosphere of confidence and a favourable climate for investment. Business began to develop in Moscow in line with world financial and economic standards. The transition period was full of shootouts and odious heroes. The Mayor successfully overcame this Chicago syndrome and remained as sole Father of the city.

In the mid-1990s Russia was seduced by freedom and underwent 'savage' privatisation. The young liberal democrats declaimed from every podium about the bourgeois happiness around the corner and citizens felt something bourgeois within themselves. The patriotic image of the national hero was replaced by the 'New Russian'. The song 'The Accountant' appeared. The country basked in happy anticipation.

It all became clear in the amazing spring of 1998. To the sound of democratic music the savages performed their favourite 'voucher' dance around a fire already burning low. When the privatisation show was over, the compere came out on stage and declared a default. Only Moscow, impervious to these erotic scenes, refused to recognise it and continued to repay its debts.

Against the background clash of ethnic conflicts the 'savage' privatisers quietly stashed everything overseas.

The pivotal moment in this idyll was Yuri Mikhailovich's announcement of the founding of the Otechestvo ('Fatherland') public movement. This reminded citizens that these things were happening in their fatherland, a land which soon might exist only in name. There was a belief that Russia and its riches should be saved. 'Yes', said the sages, 'Yuri Mikhailovich has decided to turn back the river.' And, indeed, to keep at least a bit of sanity, as the author puts it, we will have to explain this decision to ourselves solely in terms of its truly Russian character – undertake the impossible and the people's enthusiasm will catch fire.

And a miracle happened. Civic duty and courage summoned into being by one individual began to prevail over the common tendency towards enrichment without heed for the country. Otechestvo gave the call to come back to the shore of our fathers' land – noticeably emptied but still our one and only native shore. The people gave up waiting for the promised happiness, fell upon the liberal democrats themselves and, as we Russians say, twisted their tail. This did not, of course, make the rich any less wealthy, but at least it became clear what lay hidden under the liberal democrats' tail. Perhaps allegories such as this will allow us to see how great trends unfold in the popular consciousness and what role the individual plays in shaping those trends. Science tells us that a large atom forms the nucleus of a molecule and Yuri Mikhailovich, as a chunk of Russian bedrock himself, carries within him the profound wisdom of the peoples who inhabit this land, and he is generously sharing this wisdom with the English reader.

This unusual narrative genre – optimistically humorous and at the same time analytical – is a sort of management folklore. The author's aphorism, 'Getting up at five and keeping the tractor serviceable had the same relation to the business in hand as boiling bones in a cauldron has to the effectiveness of a spell' can serve as an appetiser to the content of the book, which in a certain sense reveals the secret of the Russian phenomenon. It can provide curious Europeans with a brilliant guide to our painfully different environment. It could become a bestseller or a bible for the foreign investor. And when everything starts to break down he will know that the seeds were there from the outset. But this is still not the end. There may be no end at all. Our life is a culmination. If there is a beginning it has no relation to what comes after. At first sight, this is mysticism. But this law of deviation must be factored into project calculations. So, welcome to Russia.

Ali Visaev
Journalist

Russian Parkinson's Law

DEAR FRIENDS, THE SUBJECT OF MY LECTURE is a rather unusual one. Just now everyone is talking about the crisis, the strife between the parties and the coming elections. But we are going to talk about Parkinson's Law*. Please don't mix this up with Parkinson's disease – this is a totally different Parkinson.

Now, what prompts me to address this subject at this particular moment, in these 'troubled times'? Well, it's precisely what I promised myself I was not going to mention: the crisis, the failures of reform and the other current ills. To be more exact, I want to seek out the reasons for the intolerable fact that the process of transformation has now been going on in Russia for over ten years, and, as in a fairytale, the further we go the more terrible it gets.

In the first place we have clearly underestimated the depth of the chasm between the systems and, above all, its width – I'm thinking here of those people who are so keen on leaping it.

Secondly, there are subjective factors: we have clearly been unlucky with the architects of change and the overseers of reform. I shall talk about them another time.

But there is a third reason, which has been increasingly discussed recently. Do our captains and overseers really have the right idea about just where to head and what to build? You must agree that the vision of our goal has become somewhat blurred following the débacle in August**. What seemed so clear-cut to the first wave of reformers no longer seems so.

The history of the recent financial crises has put an abrupt

---

* C Northcote Parkinson, *Parkinson's Law: The Pursuit of Progress*, (1958). A collection of laws, the most famous of which is that 'work expands to fill the time available'.

** August 1998 saw a major financial crisis in which the Russian government sharply devalued the rouble, defaulted on domestic debt and suspended foreign payments.

end to many debates. It has demonstrated, so to speak empirically, that no single template exists for a 'normal economy', no universal prescription that suits all countries. One and the same principles and programmes will produce completely different results in Japan, Germany, Korea, Indonesia and Latin America.

And as for Russia! All you can do is throw up your hands. Our dashing radical reformers operated on the premise that 'there is no need to invent anything', that 'two times two makes four both here and in Paris', as one young prime minister was fond of repeating. With a reckless perseverance these zealous youngsters copied exactly everything that was alien to local management tradition and historical habits of economic thinking and behaviour... and look what happened!

> No single template exists for a 'normal economy', no universal prescription that suits all countries.

They never did manage to answer one awkward question: if the same laws apply everywhere, then what governs the foul-ups that are distorting the reformers' good intentions out of all recognition? Whose ill-will, so to speak, is upsetting all their plans and programmes?

Instead of acknowledging the simple truth – that the failures of reform are the natural result of a cavalier attitude towards Russian realities – they have started blaming the country and its people. Some have gone so far as to assert that 'this errant country' has no right to exist, that it is a blot on the world, that its destiny is to be a black hole, to become a 'world dumping-ground' which, as one recent privatiser believes, all thinking people will be forced to leave.

And here's the strange thing. Today the entire world aspires to pluralism. The much-vaunted Western political correctness treats whites, blacks, gays, the undeveloped and the inferior as equal. You will no longer even find such a concept as 'primitive peoples' in a modern dictionary. Any aboriginal enjoys the right to live with dignity according to his own lights. The Russians alone are censured as being 'errant'; the Russians alone are not entitled to arrange their lives by their own standards.

It really is time to ask whether the general standards offered us are actually so universal. Did not Max Weber demonstrate in his *Protestant Ethic* how strictly European capitalism was conditioned by a certain mentality? Are not the entire history, ethics and traditions of Western-type civil society woven into the very fabric of the universal standards being imposed upon us?

If so, then it is also time for us at last to do the necessary work and attempt to understand how the 'enigmatic Russian character' (or mentality, in today's terms) influences and affects

the economic behaviour and business and working habits of the Russians. Without this analytical effort we cannot achieve the main objective – the building of a Russian version of a flourishing and highly productive society.

So what sort of mentality is it and how can we make it help Russia flourish? How are we to interpret the fundamental features of Russian business and work ethics?

There have been many such attempts and we are by no means trailblazers. Almost every Russian thinker, not to mention foreigner, has made a stab at a description. This exercise still remains a favourite occupation of Russians, not just at the writing desk but also at the dinner table. Indeed, I think every one of you will have a couple of witty observations stored away that you would be happy to share with the audience.

So we shall lay no claim to the laurels of a Chaadayev or a Custine, let alone of Tyutchev*, with his famous 'Russia is not to be understood with the mind…' This is, of course, a superb line. These days, however, one immediately recalls another: 'It is high time, mother-f-----s, to understand Russia with the mind'**. Guberman wrote that. Of course, it was very boorish of him to exploit freedom of speech in this far from uncontroversial way; but the idea itself is right, at least for us. Anyone who undertakes reform of the Russian social and economic system is absolutely obliged to understand it with the mind! To comprehend our own specific Russian mentality and not that of some imaginary individual, as the neo-liberals have done, pic-

---

* Petr Chaadayev (1794-1856), whose *Philosophical Letter* fiercely criticised Russian institutions; Astolphe, Marquis de Custine (1790-1857), author of the perceptive *Letters from Russia*; Fedor Tyutchev (1803-1873), Slavophile lyric poet.

** Title of a poem by Igor Guberman (b 1936), poet, writer and storyteller.

turing some abstract model moulded on the Western pattern instead of a real Russian person.

Since I am inviting you to participate in this work, I want to say right away that the features of the Russians as an ethnic group are not at issue. What we are interested in has nothing to do with either Russophobia or Russophilia. The business and working habits which we are going to consider are manifested in Russia just as much by Jews and Chechens and Germans. Conversely, when they come to the West ethnic Russians often demonstrate the ability to adapt to a different system and change as if the qualities which they show at home are not inherent but overlaid. Accordingly, we are talking not about ethnic stereotypes but rather the characteristics of a milieu, a social entity, a place in which for over a thousand years people have in essence belonged to the state, and how this has affected their business and working habits.

Are we like everyone else, only worse?

So let us restate the task. The issue which inevitably faces any administrator today is this: do we possess national features (in a broad sense) which need to be taken into account in framing a strategy for economic transformation? Or are we like everyone else, only worse? Like the Germans, only given to drunkenness. Like the Americans, only incapable of initiative. Like the Japanese, only with no capacity for work.

Why is this so important? If we are like everyone else, only spoiled by socialism, then the neo-liberals' idea of taking everything over from the West is legitimate. And the people can just get on with it and change – that's their problem. But if there are distinctive features, and important ones, then one of the reasons for the failure of reform can be seen in this method of direct borrowing.

And how are we to approach this task? I don't mean philosophers or publicists, but us, the current and future managers. How are we to understand Russia with our minds, and apply our minds to using this understanding in order to update management techniques on the basis of that understanding?

At this point the famous Parkinson's Law comes to mind, and along with it The Peter Principle, Murphy's Law and all the management folklore tradition that has grown up around them. Parkinson has lent his name to this tradition in the same way that classical physics is known as Newtonian, geometry is called Euclidean and astronomy Copernican.

I don't know how or when you read Parkinson's famous work. I read it when I was a student. Not in book form of course, but a blurred typewritten copy. That was how it was in those days – such works were known as samizdat. We lent them to each other 'for the night'. During that night I read my way through the text three times and remembered it for life. You could say it changed my outlook, gave me a point of view on situations which I encountered almost daily but had not realised were at all capable of being understood.

> These humorous laws, discovered 'somewhere over there' in the West, have proved to fit our own situation.

For some unknown reason these humorous laws, discovered 'somewhere over there' in the West, have proved to fit our own situation. Indeed, things that in the West are only exceptions, standing out against the background of the overall rational ordering of life, are familiar everyday occurrences here. So if we really must borrow management theories from the West, I would advise that we start, not with Hayek and Friedman, however good they may be, but first and foremost with Parkinson; and only move on to the others afterwards.

Look around you, read the papers, watch the television and then tell me what the outcome of applying our neo-liberals' theories most resembles – their promises, or this scientific postulate, attributed to Murphy: **'If anything can go wrong it will. If anything just cannot go wrong it will anyway.'** We see this proved every day; and isn't it true that the liberals' games, or rather their consequences under our conditions, are aptly described by the ironic formula **'left to themselves, things tend to go from bad to worse'**? I can state accurately that all of Moscow's recent achievements have been based on countering this all-pervasive axiom.

> **'If anything can go wrong it will. If anything just cannot go wrong it will anyway.'**

Parkinson did something very important when he called such ironic observations 'laws'. And you know, generally speaking, many Russian proverbs are postulates of a similar order. **'The slower you go, the farther you'll get'** – isn't that like a paradox from a book of Murphy's Law? Rephrase it in learned jargon and you could add it to the collection*. And isn't **'work is no wolf, it won't run off into the wood'** a clause from the folk labour code?

The point is, though, that folk proverbs are stylistically different. They came into being in the peasant milieu and worked there. But Parkinson's laws belong to the realm of science and the latest management practice. Formulated with playful seriousness, they have a bearing on the actual techniques of modern management.

----

* D Carnegie, L Peter, S Parkinson, A Bloch, *Your Success is in Your Own Hands*, Respublika Publications, Moscow, 1993.

> **The Persig-Luzhkov Postulate**
>
> The number of rational explanations is infinite. The number of rational actions is finite: as a rule, only one.
>
> ...from the Mayor's notepad

Would you like an example? Last week we were looking at some plans. Sadly, they were poor. I was unhappy, but I kept quiet and avoided interrupting so as not to spoil the planners' mood. Then I said, 'You know, there's this law: the product of thought multiplied by concrete is a constant'. At first they fell silent and thought about it, but then they began to smile and the penny dropped. They started to talk animatedly and suggest alternatives, and even did it enthusiastically.

What is important about this? For us practical people this sort of irony is not a mere intellectual pastime. You could come up with funnier things for the stage. But we need these laws for a specific management situation where 'metal' can easily be substituted for 'concrete', but the sense remains the same: a lot of thought means an elegant solution; little thought means enormous material inputs.

Today I am inviting you to join in working on the code of Russian Parkinson's Law. There is a good deal of scope for wit in this work; but some restraint has to be exercised, for the point is not laughter but utility. We need memorable, meaningful formulations that will help us better understand the result we can expect from the application of particular management techniques. I'll explain right away.

Let us recall how Murphy's Law came into being. As you will know, its progenitor was no humorist, but an ordinary engineer and, by all accounts, a great nitpicker. Otherwise the fact that equipment was being wrongly assembled would have made less of an impression on him. I mean, big deal! It happens thousands of times. But Ed Murphy just started going up and pestering everyone, saying 'You know, if there is any way of assembling it wrong, then they will.' And he went on at them so much that the project manager eventually confessed to journalists, 'We owe our success to overcoming Murphy's Law'. There's the key word: 'overcoming'. Therein lies the essence of our entire management technique. We must formulate laws that enable us to foresee how the outcome may be distorted while we are still at the stage of stating the task.

> Ed Murphy:
> 'You know, if there is any way of assembling it wrong, then they will.'

The law of
Inevitable Distortions

or

'We wanted the best, but it turned out as always'

You will probably remember this story: at a Russian factory they started making mincers, ladles and other domestic utensils, but do what they would, they always ended up with a Kalashnikov.

The funniest thing about this is that it's absolutely true to life. At one time I was involved in designing analytical test instruments for the chemical industry. A colleague of mine, Nikolai Yakovlevich Festa, had to keep going to Tula*, where a branch of our institute was being built. One day he comes back and he says, 'You know what's amazing? Everything they design there, all the instruments, all the sensors, look like the bolt of an assault rifle. It's just astonishing: the final configuration of any instrument, whatever its function, is an exact copy of a bolt.' So I go there and I look, and he's quite right! And so I formulated to myself this 'bolt law', as it was originally known.

This is the most universal of all the laws in the Russian Parkinson's Law Code. Of course, it found its classic statement in the words of our former prime minister**: 'We wanted the best, but it turned out as always'. There's no point now in trying to better this formula. It has entered the golden treasury of Russian management folklore. You could inscribe it on the pediments of government buildings. Today it is our most quoted saying.

● ●

* The centre of Russia's firearms industry, where the Kalashnikov assault rifle is made.
** Viktor Chernomyrdin, prime minister from 1993 to 1998.

This goes to show that work has already begun on formulating our 'Parkinson's Law'. So far, to be sure, it has happened spontaneously: such sentences simply tripped off our old leaders' tongues. Journalists only had to capture and disseminate them. Now, with your assistance, we have to ensure that truths like this become part of universal literacy and enter the school textbooks. For, as we know, ignorance of the law is no excuse.

The law of inevitable distortions manifests itself most vividly when we work from borrowed models. We try to make an exact replica and end up with something that makes foreigners' heads spin. They say they've never seen anything like it. And we can't understand, because we think you simply can't tell the two apart. Take the present tax system. It is based on the best models, but they tell us there is nothing like it anywhere in the world.

This has always been the way in Russian history. It happened both after Peter the Great's reforms and after Lenin's revolution. And it's happening now: the more we have of capitalism and the market based on Friedman's and the IMF's prescriptions, the more Russian feudalism there is in practice. We tried to build a market economy and got a 'bluffonomy'. We tried to achieve free competition and built a system in which the bulk of profit derives not from market success, but from the allocation of 'income through power', the ability to get on with those in authority, exploit unofficial understandings and so on. It's the same old story, the same old pattern, and the same old rifle bolt.

> We tried to build a market economy and got a 'bluffonomy'.

Could we have foreseen this? Of course we could. Should we have taken this as a starting premise? Of course we should. Because the current system is not just a random deviation from the 'correct' market model. It has moulded itself to our experience, to our traditions, traditions which only the descendants of Saltykov-Shchedrin's Glupovites* could have ignored when planting a market economy. (If you remember, the people of Glupov likewise scattered grain on unploughed land, saying 'The damn stuff will come up on its own!').

It was as though the architects of our current situation were unaware that the Soviet authorities had been bluffing, only pretending that we had a wholly planned system. As though they had never heard that plans couldn't be fulfilled without using informal contacts, barter and other underground mechanisms. As if they had never in their lives seen the black market, or wholesale thieving or any of the other delights of Soviet amateur economic activity.

Planning was merely an outer covering for the system, like a tortoise's shell, so that when the new market features – exchanges, brokers, shares and whatever – took its place, little changed in the actual dualistic set-up. The quasi-market structures began to rely for survival on the same old underground machinery and economic relationships began to rely on informal ones. What we got in practice was not open, law-based relations, but an increase in clannishness, paternalism and diktat by regional government – the birthmarks

> The people of Glupov scattered grain on unploughed land, saying 'The damn stuff will come up on its own!'

---

* Reference to the novel *History of a Town* by the satirist Mikhail Saltykov-Shchedrin (1826-1889). Glupov, the eponymous town, roughly means 'Idiotville'.

of stagnation. We got all those things that are shaped not by purely economic conditions and the corresponding legal norms, but solely by the need to survive in this environment. Nobody can yet tell where the market is in this set-up, which bits are remnants of socialism and which are some other thing. I call this system a 'bluffonomy', but we will talk about that another time.

> We do know that two and two are four; but we still need to get there.

What are we to do? Surely we are not going to give up on a free economy just because we don't know how to make the transition. Of course not. But if we understand how the system functions, using quasi-market clothing as camouflage, then we shall probably learn how to master it. For, despite the enormous number of distortions that shape our economic life, we can already find a great many parts of it which operate according to market

Hanlon's Postulate

Never attribute to malice that which can be adequately explained by stupidity.

...from the Mayor's notepad

principles. They may not work too well, but they do work; it may be hard, but they keep going. It's these that we should study, encourage and clone, seeking to disseminate and make dominant their working practices and the ethics they apply to relationships.

Our task is a bit like a school textbook with the answers at the back. We do know that two and two are four; but we still need to get there.

The law of Compulsory Cheating

or

'If you don't infringe you can't sleep'

Play on a Russian proverb.

I USED TO HAVE A DRIVER, an honest fellow, who had worked for me for a long time. One evening he's driving me home after work and he says, 'I won't sleep tonight.' 'Why's that?' 'Well... I have problems sleeping anyway. But, you know, I've noticed that if I don't break the traffic rules for a whole day, I can't get to sleep for anything!'

Believe me, I couldn't suspect him of being abnormal. He was an absolutely healthy Russian lad. And then, as I remember, I thought, could you imagine a Westerner, say a German, saying something like that? He wouldn't even go through a red light when there's nothing coming. 'So', I asked, 'are you telling me you break them every day?' 'Yeah. I can't help it. But I do sleep afterwards.' And that is how the Law of Compulsory Cheating entered my collection.

> 'Filch from the factory every screw, Remember, it belongs to you!'

We all know it in a range of guises. **'Filch from the factory every screw, / Remember, it belongs to you!'** If you think it's just modern poetry, have a look at Dal's dictionary (1863-66): **'Steal public property as if you were saving it from fire. Public property is there to give us a living.'** And here's a particularly heartfelt one: **'We are all Mother Russia's children, she's our mother, so we'll suck from her.'**

How far is this greed and how far habit? Can we really talk, for example, about petty pilfering in legal terms? People don't feel right if they don't take something from the factory. And whether the factory has been floated or privatised doesn't matter. And those around them wouldn't understand. I remember, back in the old Moscow Council days there would be endless arguments with the police: 'Why don't you combat petty theft?' 'Yuri Mikhailovich', would come the answer, 'we can't jail everybody!'

Recently I met an expert in tax collection. 'The big difficulty', he said, 'is not that people want to evade taxes. That happens worldwide. It's that they enjoy doing it.' Do you know what is going on here? The most honest workman, who will teach his children not to steal and would never take anything belonging to another, regards it as his downright duty to cheat the state, steal from the factory and avoid paying taxes. Most importantly, this is not condemned by society. Because we have a double standard of honesty. One philosophy applies to neighbours, another to the state and the factory (which somehow seems to belong to them). And the state knows this. It, so to speak, incorporates legal infringements in its prescriptions. It pays the official a pittance in the expectation that he will look after himself. It introduces taxes that it would be inconceivable to pay. It creates a set of contradictory laws that it is impossible not to break.

> 'The big difficulty is not that people want to evade taxes... It's that they enjoy doing it.'

Our fellow citizens look on the law roughly as they do on winter boots: they assess it from the point of view of comfort. The very idea that the law must be obeyed regardless is incomprehensible in our heart of hearts. When it is inconvenient or unfair, we say, 'Let's change the law, because people made it! And people get things wrong.' And we hope – no, we are sure – we shall be understood.

In olden times in Russia they used to say, **'Let all laws perish as long as people live right'**. That is our ideal. Do you remember that bit in Ostrovskiy's* play? 'Men', asks the landowner, 'how shall I judge you, according to the law or

---

* Aleksandr Ostrovskiy (1823-86), major dramatist.

according to conscience?' 'According to conscience!' reply the peasants. That's to say, fairly. To them – and indeed to us – that seems more right and easier to understand.

What sort of tradition is this and what is to be done about it? Does it not testify to some tacit common conspiracy against all authority? Perhaps authority and the state, however constituted, are perceived in the public consciousness as inherently hostile?

What I would say is this. We see here two interrelated tendencies, two propensities in Russian people: the need for a leader, a tsar, strong supreme authority, and the absolute need to deceive that authority. These are complementary things.

The ideal condition of such a system is that there should be a tsar who isn't very clever, who needs to be praised, tripped up, have various crises foisted on him and generally be thwarted in every way. He must be responsible for everything and have no idea what to do. And under the shelter of this tsar-cum-leader-cum-idol people should be able to get on with their business, not according to the law, but in accordance with a tacit understanding, the unwritten rules which embody the common principle of Russian everyday life: 'Live and let live'.

> 'The severity of Russian law is softened by the fact that compliance is optional.'

Since we are interested in the consequences of all this for management, let us not forget to add this well-known postulate to our list of Parkinson's laws: **'The severity of Russian law is softened by the fact that compliance is optional.'**

Let us look at this in detail.

The classic management method is based on the assumption that orders will be obeyed more or less to the letter. This method has lots of merits, but on one condition: orders must be ration-

> ### The Russian way with the law
>
> If you mustn't but you need to, then you can.
>
> ...from the Mayor's notepad

al, for with incompetent management this practice will quickly lead to the breakdown of the system. In Russia a different practice obtains: each individual order is ill obeyed, but the system as a whole is accordingly more stable, because it has adapted to survive in a climate of bad management. I remember back in the 1960s Khrushchev told all the collective farms to sow maize. If something like that had happened in the West, where officials operate on classic lines, the consequences would have been disastrous. But here nothing happened. Everybody saluted, but nobody even thought of taking the order seriously.

> Khrushchev told all the collective farms to sow maize... everybody saluted, but nobody even thought of taking the order seriously.

And note that the system is surviving on the same pattern now. When our radical reformers decided to introduce the market at a stroke, the system reacted roughly as it had to Khrushchev's maize. Laws were passed instantly; reports were sent to the IMF that a market economy was already flourishing in Russia, with wholesale privatisation, stock exchanges, bankruptcies and no end of arrests. But in fact the exchanges weren't really exchanges, and privatisation was associated least of all with the idea of an owner, and bankruptcies were little more than a way of redistributing property. I won't even mention such concepts as infrastructure, let alone market ethics.

Thanks to the postulate 'If you don't infringe you can't sleep', utopia in our country easily turns into reality, changing out of all recognition in the process. And no IMF will ever realise that this new, transformed reality does not just boil down to criminality and corruption, as people, rushing to the other extreme, are now trying to portray it. It remains precisely a reality, that is – something that requires careful handling and, above all, understanding.

> 'If you don't infringe you can't sleep.'

Because the authorities, if they want to achieve anything within this system, must first of all remember that they are dealing with a special 'object of control' that has been taught over many years to trust no authority. This means that the key task is first and foremost to gain that trust in order to lead society... yes, to the market, where else?

The law of
'No, it's impossible'

or

'The best way of burying a problem'

The cartoon alludes to a tale in which everyone in a peasant household, including the dog, cat and mouse, has to join in before they can pull up a miraculous giant turnip. The moral is that collective effort is rewarded. In this case all they get is a giant hand giving the Russian equivalent of two fingers.

I FORMULATED THIS LAW THE FIRST TIME I VISITED THE WEST. I was struck by the fact that when you set people there a problem they would immediately think how to solve it. Following set patterns of course, without our Russian native wit and inventiveness. But most importantly, their mindset is to resolve any – even the most complicated – issue.

Over the centuries we have nurtured a different philosophy. If a problem is raised, reasons need to be found not to solve it. The current transition to the market makes no difference. 'Impossible' is the sweetest word in the Russian business lexicon. You haven't finished talking when they're already replying, 'No, it won't work'.

But why exactly? Well, in the highest spheres you can see why: there, if you solve a problem, you put yourself at risk. Someone may not like it. This is well reflected in the sayings 'Don't put yourself forward', 'What makes you so different?', 'Don't push in before your betters' and so on. It's also beneficial to fail to make a decision, or to refuse under whatever pretext: someone around you will have to make a move, perhaps give a kickback or do something for you. And you are showing that you're a big boss. But of course the real fun comes when your job lets you stop someone else doing what he desperately needs to, and you can accept a present for no longer getting in the way.

All this, however, applies to officialdom and to the high up and seems clear enough. But why does the Law of 'No' operate in what we call the real world? I can't see for the life of me.

It is awesome how much effort a Russian will put into something he has no intention of doing. He'll come to see you, ask questions, confer, look, consider options. But it doesn't mean

> 'Impossible' is the sweetest word in the Russian business lexicon.

he intends to solve your problem. He may even waste more time than it would take to get the thing done. But, as the saying goes, your health is more important.

The Law of 'No' is so wide-ranging and diverse in practice that we could devote a lecture to it on its own. I think – though I can't understand it fully, because it is so alien to my character – that it works like this. Russians are accustomed to giving the name 'problem' only to problems that have no solution. Instead of identifying the most important

> It is awesome how much effort a Russian will put into something he has no intention of doing.

issues and tackling them first, they usually do the reverse. They build up the problem to the point where it becomes insoluble. You can see this even at the domestic level. You call in a

---

Chisholm's Enigma

When you are sure everyone will like what you do, they are sure not to.

...from the Mayor's notepad

plumber to fix a tap and he says right away, 'No, it's impossible. There's no washer, no screw, no valve, and anyway I'd need to take out the bathtub.' Do you think it's just greed, that he wants to push up the price and get an extra bottle out of the customer? If only! These are just explanations we use to comfort ourselves and keep at least a bit of sanity. Globalising problems and thereby burying them is the first reaction of Russian people and, most importantly, an almost unconscious one. It's a habit, a culture, a ritual.

Many leaders and politicians, however, exploit this quite consciously. What is interesting is that everyone falls in with them. One day I was taught this method by the same Nikolai Yakovlevich Festa whom I mentioned earlier. At the time we were engaged in introducing computerised monitoring into a chemical production facility. I ran into problems with ammonia: the processes were hazardous and the computers poor. And I decided to hold back for the time being. So at a meeting I said it was too early and I was against it. Nobody understood, and they put me down as a young stick-in-the-mud. I remember Festa took me aside and read me a lecture. 'You're right, but you went about it the wrong way. You should have said the opposite: yes, comrades, it's great. Computers are opening up tremendous prospects. Soon we'll be able to entrust them not just with monitoring, but also with optimisation, information and control. Let's decide right now to start preparing this massive programme... Now if you'd built up the problem like that, everyone would have been in favour and the thing would have died a natural death.'

> Globalising problems and thereby burying them is the first reaction of Russian people.

The law of
Avos*

or

'The principle of optimal expectations'

* Translator's note: The Russian word avos expresses irrational hope based on inadequate foundations. As the author states, no translation can fully capture its nuances, but the translation 'with luck' is used here to give the basic idea.

We're talking here about the Russian way of decision-making. Science tells us that when there is little data and a lot of risk, there are two ways of making decisions. With the first, known as the minimax method, you analyse all the possible values of the uncertainty factors and make a decision based on the least unfavourable combination.

With the second (it's called risk minimisation) you take into account the probability of the different variants of a situation and act on the basis of what one might call mathematical expectation.

But in Russia there is this third method, which we have never come across in serious scientific papers. It could also be termed The Law of Risk Optimisation.

The decision is sought by expecting the best possible outcome from the uncertainty factors, applying the principle: **'With luck *(avos)* it will work out!'**

It is hard even to assess what sort of risk people run when they make decisions on this basis. The number of people who have died and who, God forbid, are still to die from acting on this principle has yet to be counted. Although, to be fair, it has to be admitted that precisely this approach has sometimes produced the unique achievements and discoveries in which Russian history abounds.

> I once used it in a lecture in America. The interpreter racked her brains, came up with something on the lines of 'maybe yes, maybe no', and then said, 'No, they wouldn't understand anyway, it isn't for Americans'.

'Russians were raised on *avos*', says a folk proverb, and we know what it means. But it is a word that cannot be translated properly into any other language. I once used it in a lecture in

> **Meskimen's Law**
>
> There's never time to do it right, but there's always time to do it over.
>
> ...from the Mayor's notepad

America. The interpreter racked her brains, came up with something on the lines of 'maybe yes, maybe no', and then said, 'No, they wouldn't understand anyway, it isn't for Americans.'

We don't like to think through consequences – **'Russians sit firm on three pillars: with luck, probably and somehow'** – even amidst the unending defaults and cataclysms in which our current life is so rich.

30

The law of
Everything Now

or

'The principle of ultimate states'

Allusion to Aesop's fable of the fox and the crow.

You are well aware what I'm talking about: this is the principle we applied in nationalising in 1917 and privatising in 1992. And note that this was done by different people who agreed on almost nothing. Yet the style is the same. This means that there's nothing individual about it. It also means that our neo-liberals are one flesh with the people, whatever they may think and whatever they may read in 'imported' languages.

> 'Break, don't build' – there's our motto. All our efforts go into destruction.

At one time almost the whole of Europe was chorusing, 'Get down to the basics and then...' But for them it was no more than a metaphor, an invitation to join a trend, as it were. For us it is something literal and as inevitable as fate.

Gattuso's Postulate

Nothing is ever so bad that it can't get worse.

...from the Mayor's notepad

'Break, don't build' – there's our motto. All our efforts go into destruction. Neither strength nor organisation are left for creating. We love to break things! Nobody needs to be asked. Nobody ever argues. Whenever the need to destroy has arisen, I don't ever remember encountering difficulties. Work organisation is ideal; enthusiasm is total; there is no end of willing hands. Even the planners usually have to be reined in: they want to get rid of all irregularities and level the landscape. 'How does that hillock get in your way?' I'll ask, 'and see what a nice little dell that is, let's use it.' But no. The basic tendency is to leave nothing and start from zero every time.

It's after that the difficulties and argy-bargy begin. If we have thought of something massive, we are capable of undreamt-of feats. We are capable as nobody else of a one-off effort. Reverse the flow of rivers – we can do that. Build enormous cities in the permafrost – certainly. Plough up a million hectares of virgin land* – no problem. And do you know what's amazing? I worked on the virgin lands and I can tell you.

It would seem a vast undertaking, ploughing the steppes where nothing but weeds have ever grown. You would think it would mean planning, checking, parcelling out into plots, making adjustments... Not a bit of it. That bores us. We don't like doing things that way. It doesn't inspire us. The mindset was completely different: to plough and sow it all at a stroke, and all in the same way!

> The mindset was completely different: to plough and sow it all at a stroke, and all in the same way!

---

* Reference to Krushchev's plan of the 1950s to bring vast new tracts of land under cultivation.

'Things will look after themselves' – that's our faith.
'It will work, it has to' – that's our magical belief.

So, although you had to get up at five and fix the tractor and work until night-time, somehow none of that had a direct bearing on the result. The result was not built up to, but appeared by magic. And so getting up at five and keeping the tractor serviceable had the same relation to the business in hand as boiling bones in a cauldron has to the effectiveness of a spell.

But, you will say, that all happened under the Communists. For you, of course, that belongs to days long gone. Fine, then let's move on to more recent times, when the need arose to accomplish the country's transition from socialism to a post-industrial state.

> According to Academician Pontryagin, optimal management lies somewhere between 'full steam ahead' and 'full speed reverse'.

Other countries would have looked at it like this: we are facing an enormous shake-up; we need to reshape the entire structure, create tens of millions of new jobs, and do it over a vast area. The process will have to be drawn out over at least twenty years. And what is twenty years? The life of an entire generation. That means we need to think through everything carefully and contrive matters so that people can live relatively normally over that time and find existence tolerable during the transition period. Is that hard to do? Yes, but it's possible. At least we can set ourselves the task, and at least we can try.

Nothing remotely like that happened. Once again they sought to make the leap at one go, in a single bound, from the ultra-centralised Soviet economy to an equally extreme version of a liberal market economy. Not gradually but all at once. So, you see, the system has changed but the Law of Everything Now continues to operate. Its roots lie deeper than the social system, and how to delve down to it is still a big problem.

Incidentally, with this proclivity, social processes can occur much more quickly than in other countries. According to

This cartoon alludes to a well-known Russian fairytale, The Tale of the Golden Fish. *An old fisherman catches a magical fish that promises to grant his wishes if he will let it go. The old man releases the fish, but asks no reward, and is only later induced by his shrewish wife to make increasingly extravagant demands. Here, however, in a dig at the Russian character, the fisherman has sought instant gratification by demanding a barrel of beer, and swills it down without any thought for the hapless fish.*

Academician Pontryagin*, optimal management lies somewhere between 'full steam ahead' and 'full speed reverse'. In any other civilised environment you could just tell people to follow the middle line, but that will not do for the Russian character. Right now, right here and at once – that's our way. And then the same thing in reverse. You could call it the method of conflicting high demands. But it can work if it is used cleverly and, above all, with exquisite precision.

This law has many corollaries which I will not go into now. I will mention only the **Principle of Manna from Heaven**, ie a sort of aspiration to a state of effortless bliss that starts tomorrow. It pervades our entire folklore and history. Remember those fairytales: sometimes a pike jumps out of a hole in the ice and instantly shells out more than you could save by the time you retired in other countries; sometimes the stove cooks tasty dishes of its own accord, and Ivanushka or Yemelya lie there at ease, spitting at the ceiling. Or a rich foreign lady falls in love with the hero, albeit in the guise of a frog. Or a golden fish swims up and asks, 'What do you want, old man?'

Wealth is never directly connected with effort or subject to worldly laws. You think that's just in fairytales? And what about how we debate the budget and want someone to find the money this instant, in a way that means no taxes need to be paid and spending can be increased – isn't this also a fairytale?

---

* Lev Pontryagin (1908-88), mathematician.

The law of
By and Large
or
'The principle of compulsory non-completion'

WHO IS IT WHO NEVER GETS ROUND TO FINISHING THE REPAIRS, DEAR?

PEOPLE IN RUSSIA LOVE ALL SORTS OF NEW INITIATIVES. As Mayor I am always being invited to First Congresses. And do you know what I have noticed? Second congresses are a great rarity, and third ones even more.

We adore beginnings, but it is utterly impossible to get anything finished. Builders have long since formulated their own 'Parkinson's Law': **'Repairs can never be completed; they can only be stopped.'** Put in more general terms, the law goes like this: **'It is possible somehow to get 95% of a job completed. The last 5% almost never.'**

It is as though some diabolical force prevents us from doing a thing properly and putting the finishing touches. It may not be by much, but we won't quite get there. It may only be 5%, but we'll leave something undone. But you see, as a rule, it is just this last 5% that means quality!

I have just been looking carefully at this 'rough-and-ready' principle in the context of the revival of Moscow's vehicle plants. It is operating faultlessly. And not just as regards the end result, oh no: at every stage and in every component something is not quite finished, and the tiniest rough edges, maladjustments and imperfections are left. We build an engine that in conceptual terms is as good as its German counterpart, but we can't be bothered to get it just right.

> 'Repairs can never be completed; they can only be stopped.'

I ask them, who's stopping you? And I can see that the factory worker just doesn't get it. He'll nod, he'll agree, but to him what I'm talking about is just a minor detail. His look says, 'There's a connecting rod, a piston, piston rings, a cylinder block – what more do you want?' And it's not a matter of skill (he could shoe a flea) or technological illiteracy, but something else. It's a vision of the goal, based on that same troublesome 'with luck', 'probably' and 'somehow'.

I once had a Zaporozhets car. I had a dreadful time with it; I had to keep taking the engine apart every month. One day in wintertime when I had the leisure what I decided to do was this: I dismantled the engine and weighed all the identical parts – pistons, connecting rods and so on – and I saw that the weights didn't match. So I ground and I filed, and I put it back together again. I started up, and I was amazed: the engine purred like a Singer sewing machine. Who was stopping them doing that at the factory? Now we know: it was the universal effect of this law.

I'm always asking doctors why our patients are afraid to have operations here. Because we have unique surgeons, fantastic ones. Where a Western surgeon, accustomed to relying on sophisticated technology, would be at a loss, our surgeons will come up with a novel solution, find a way out, dream something up. So why at the first opportunity do people go where, unless you're insured, all this stuff is ludicrously expensive? I ask them, but I already know the answer. Yes, the surgeon will perform a brilliant operation. But then the pretty nurse will fail to adjust the drip or old Vasya, suffering from his morning hangover, will forget to replace the oxygen cylinder. That's the long and the short of it. You'd think there was no comparison between producing a good surgeon and making a system run efficiently. But we can't manage. It won't behave. As long as you keep your hands on it, it works, but just let it go and everything goes back to its old ways.

> The surgeon will perform a brilliant operation... old Vasya, suffering from his morning hangover, will forget to replace the oxygen cylinder.

Russians prefer a spasmodic all-out unique one-off effort at the limits of their physical abilities to monotonous routine work, even if it is more lucrative and involves less strain. We find a special Saturday when everyone turns out preferable to clearing up rubbish every day.

The **Makeshift Law** can be regarded as a special case of this. It is very similar to Meskimen's principle: **'There's never time to do it right, but there's always time to do it over.'** That formula is taken from the 'Murphy's Law' collection. It looks like a universal principle, but in fact there's a fundamental difference: over there it's a psychological trait, here it's a culture.

We knock everything together anyhow, as if temporarily – laws, roads, apartment blocks, always so that afterwards it needs to be remodelled and repaired; so that things have to be done afresh each time, instead of doing things properly once.

'Akulya, Akulya, why are you putting the stitches in the wrong place? – Never mind, Mummy, I can unpick them again!'

Nowhere but Russia, I believe, could such a saying have become widespread and generally understood.

We could go on formulating the laws of our mentality. It's an uncommonly entertaining pastime.

I should have liked, for example, to talk in more detail about the **Law of Extremes**. This has long been crystallised in popular sayings: 'All or nothing', 'Either a lord or a lost man', 'Neck or nothing', 'Either shatter the woman or split the man'. (The last one is, of course, a euphemism, but I'm no ethnographer to go quoting popular expressions uncensored.)

> We knock everything together anyhow... so that afterwards it needs to be remodelled and repaired.

These aren't just some ancient examples from an anthology of Russian sayings. A propensity to extremes in our words and deeds is an age-old trait which I have to control not just in my staff but even in myself. And when it comes to politicians, decisions based on this principle are particularly convincing and enjoy universal support. And that, as you will realise, is a great temptation.

Then there's a law which I call **'...And Eternal Battle'*** or the **Law of Perpetual Strife**, whereby we seek to solve problems by fighting rather than working. Instead of everyone getting down to it in their own place (and there is room enough for everyone) and putting our troubled country into order, people engage in constant strife and witch hunts, bug and bribe in quest of compromising material, denounce enemies and trade accusations. 'In struggle you will make your name'** is the anthem not just of our politicians, but regrettably of many of our executives, too. The country has been shaken by all of this for years now.

I still have a lot of laws left, but sadly no time to dwell on them. For example, there's the **Zone Law**, which has to do with the fact that we have fences everywhere and they all have holes in them. Or there's the **Bath-House Law**, which is about the Russian ways of dealing with problems in an informal setting. Or then there's the very important principle of what you might call work incentives Russian-style: **'Drudge away and they'll take it from you, swing the lead and they'll forgive you.'** Until recently it seemed this principle would disappear with socialism, but in fact, as Vysotskiy*** sang, 'No, lads, it's still not right, it's still not right, my lads!' The system has changed, but the mind-

---

* Reference to a famous line from the poem 'On the field of Kulikovo' by Aleksandr Blok (1880-1921).
** A slogan (rather than song) of the Left Socialist Revolutionaries, a small party briefly in coalition with the Bolsheviks after the October Revolution.
*** Vladimir Vysotskiy (1938-80), poet and singer.

set has stayed the same. So just you decide what is primary here, and what secondary: the social system or Russian Parkinson's Law.

The basic conclusion is clear. Everyone complains nowadays that we don't live according to the law. That's wrong. We do. But it's Parkinson's.

And now, my friends, if you'll attend for a little longer, let's stop and think what the purpose of this work of ours is.

This by the way, is a habit that it's useful to develop. IBM once gave me a souvenir, a little plaque inscribed 'Think!' At first I paid it no attention. I put it on my desk and forgot it. But over time I began to notice that this silent presence was somehow affecting my decision-making. It stood there, apparently unnoticed, but kept on drumming something into you. You would recall papers you'd already signed, think again and look for options. It proved very useful.

A comment on inflation.

So, to continue. Everything we've been saying so far has been a bit like a satire: the Westerners seem normal enough, but over here we're bad – we lie on the stove and wait to default. Of course, it's fine to be able to laugh at yourself, but only up to a point. Ultimately we are talking about the same people who once, living in the harshest natural conditions, managed to rise from a collection of princedoms devastated by the Mongol Tartars into a mighty power occupying a sixth of the world's land mass and playing an extremely significant geopolitical role. We are talking about the people who, almost in our own time (or anyway in the lifetime of my generation) managed, in the midst of a raging war, to relocate industry beyond the Urals in a few months and to step up annual production of tanks to 30,000 and aircraft to 40,000 in two years. This is no ordinary people.

> The problem, then, is not that Russia is a country with inferior people, but that today it is an ill-run country. That is the snag.

The problem, then, is not that Russia is a country with inferior people, but that today it is an ill-run country. That is the snag.

In general terms, control is only possible when you know what consequences your controlling action will produce; when, as in the proverb, you reap as you sow. If you sowed one thing and something completely different came up, it would send any leader mad. You might as well turn out the light, give up and die.

But isn't that how we're living today? We invest money to stimulate production and spawn parasitic middlemen. We bankrupt an enterprise run according to all the rules and line the pockets of swindlers and corrupt officials. We regulate taxes and encourage undeclared holdings of 'black cash'. And it's like that in everything: science is impotent, prescriptions don't help, and expert recommendations have exactly the opposite effect to that intended.

But yet the people who said, 'Give us a free market and everything will be just as in the developed countries' were no fools. Nor were they raving when they promised that privatisation would put a stop to thieving. Nor was it madmen who told us we should hand everything to private entrepreneurs and then the market would do the rest. No, these were educated, well-read people who were familiar with world practice. And indeed the world rallied to our aid. The best foreign consultants came to measure us up for the classic models. Experts from the IMF rigorously monitored all the government's actions. And what is the upshot? Instead of financial stabilisation, we have unheard-of economic and legal miracles – in the sense that they break all the laws of nature. Monetarism without money, structural overhaul without investment. And, on top of it all, we are up to our eyes in debt.

> 'I'll plant nothing but weeds and let the vegetables crowd them out!'

Note that I am not talking now about wrongdoing, criminal privatisation, the illegal expatriation of money or deliberate deception by 'consultants'. All these things need to be looked at – reversed, stopped, reviewed. Fine. We can see that. But then what? Should we do everything over in reverse, as in the story about the gardener whose vegetables wouldn't grow because of the weeds. 'Next year,' he decided, 'I'll plant nothing but weeds and let the vegetables crowd them out!' This is roughly what our extreme left semi-defenders of the people are suggesting. But of course we can't go down that road.

So let us go back to that plaque inscribed 'Think!'

Classic management science is based on ideas going back to Macchiavelli, as a source of positive knowledge, a storehouse of secrets and recommendations: you'll succeed if you do so-and-so and so-and-so. Open any of your management handbooks and it's full of advice. You can find techniques, models, graphs and calculations for effectiveness. But it is all designed for standard situations. When a deviation occurs, efforts are directed exclusively to re-establishing the norm. Classic management makes no provision for warped, irregular states in which the very machinery of cause and effect breaks down. Everything is geared to the typical situation, the standard and the norm.

Of course, this sort of management is useful and you have to study it. But here's the snag: in order for such rational principles to work you first need to establish a system in which they can work – where everything is cut and dried, where you stop when you brake, turn when you swing round the steering wheel, and know what a signal means when you see it. Now, my brother Arkadiy taught me to drive. 'See that clown ahead signalling left?' he would say. 'Which way do you think he's going to turn – left? You'd be a fool if you thought so, and you'd smash up the car at the next crossroads.' That's just how we need to think today.

The experts may make allowances for local peculiarities, but for them they're just another factor. All the same, they say, the ABC of the market is immutable: investment, taxes and marketing. But the fact that investment will go missing en route, 'black cash' holdings can't be taxed and marketing will be stymied by Russia's mafia doesn't fit in with the classical principles.

> The fact that investment will go missing en route, 'black cash' holdings can't be taxed and marketing will be stymied by Russia's mafia doesn't fit in with the classical principles.

And today it is just these things that characterise our Russian economic world. Something has happened to the very idea of following rules. No link can be discerned between cause and effect. It is unclear what is permissible and what isn't, what may happen and what may not. There is no set of checks and standards, but instead an almost nonsensical mishmash to which it is impossible to apply a rational positivist approach.

And this is where we come back to Parkinson's discovery and the whole tradition that has arisen from it of creating ironic laws.

Of course, when Sir Cyril Northcote Parkinson conceived his famous study, the last thing in his mind was that he was creating a management revolution. Serious scholars are still unable to accept the importance of his discoveries. They regard them as a joke, as management humour, and only on those terms are willing to read and praise him. He is known here, and indeed everywhere else, as a satirist, a writer of pamphlets that are designed to amuse the public rather than describe something that deserves serious attention.

But in fact we are dealing with a principle which has turned classical theory upside down and begun a new round in its development. Parkinson taught us to see things not in a standard but in an ironic light. With him a vital strand made its way into management science in the guise of 'fun': he legitimised irregular phenomena which we had previously only been able to perceive as violations and

> **Parkinson taught us to see things not in a standard but in an ironic light.**

The universal work input paradox

The first 90% of a project takes 10% of the time, the last 10% takes the rest.

...from the Mayor's notepad

made them permissible. He took the science beyond the confines of the classic system, in which there is one right model and all the rest are wrong. Thanks to this viewpoint, situations which had been pronounced abnormal have become fit to exist. They may not be good, but at least we know they are natural and have therefore to be adapted to somehow in order for life to go on more or less normally from day to day.

Parkinson's Law is similar to the quantum revolution in physics. Skipping the necessary caveats, we can put it like this. These laws emphasise the very idea of cause and effect. They have been introduced on the 'complementarity principle', to use an expression of Nils Bohr's. Underlying them is another, irrational world, in which, as in *Alice Through the Looking Glass*, the rules of the game change while you are playing and you never know where the next piece of mischief is coming from.

> 'If you throw it away, you will need it the next day.'

Let's ask ourselves seriously what is the basis of Richard's Postulate that

'If you keep anything long enough, you can throw it away. If you throw it away, you will need it the next day.'

It's useless to ask, it's not a matter of causes. That's just how life is. What scientific law underlies the observation that **Troubles never come singly**? There is no answer. But unfortunately it works impeccably.

When I was still a director I always applied Klipstein's Law: **'The firmness of delivery dates is inversely proportional to the tightness of the schedule'** and it never failed. Or there was Stockmayer's Theorem: **'If it looks easy it will be tough.'** And it's true. Never once did things turn out otherwise.

What kind of laws are these? These are laws not of cause but of tendency; not of statistics but of situation; not of physics but of fate. But they are laws. But on a different level. But they work. But we don't know how... As you see, I have fallen into Zhvanetskiy's logic: 'but little ones, but three'*. And that is natural, because he found a way to express the same idea: in Russia today we are living in an illogical world and only aspire to having this absurd life recognised as being as valid as any other – simply because it is the only one we have.

Of course, our objective is to achieve a system where everything would work on its own, almost without the intervention of the authorities; where transmission mechanisms would not break down nor driving belts fail, and outcomes would correspond to intentions.

> Our objective is to build a system in which all the habits, qualities and traditions of the Russian people operate as a plus rather than a minus.

Our objective is to build a system in which all the habits, qualities and traditions of the Russian people operate as a plus rather than a minus. The Japanese accomplished a similar objective in the past, and China is now very effectively demonstrating a version of its own.

I will not talk about our vision of such a system. We have been discussing this for a long time now, including in *Otechestvo's*** publications, and anyone who is interested can read about it. We are talking about something else just now.

---

* Quotation from a poem 'I saw some crayfish' by the satirist and humorous writer, Mikhail Zhvanetskiy (b 1934), in which phrase after phrase begins with 'but'.

** Otechestvo ('Fatherland') is the political movement led by Yuri Luzhkov.

This future system cannot be designed in the abstract, according to a template, precisely because we are dealing with as yet unidentified 'Parkinson's laws à la Russe'.

Yes, a programme is necessary, we cannot do without one. One of the failings of previous governments, for which we have criticised them, is that they lacked any clear-cut programme making it possible to identify priorities, achieve staged progress and check the results. All that is true. But in our conditions we need to remember that any programme can only be implemented on a step-by-step basis, where you take a step, see the result and adjust the next one accordingly, and where, at the same time, you must keep the whole thing in mind and amend your plan while concrete action is in progress.

> We are dealing with as yet unidentified 'Parkinson's laws à la Russe'.

Do you know what management is like in a time of transition? It is like walking a tightrope over a chasm: you have to keep moving all the time. As soon as you stop you fall off.

When a system has yet to gel, when it is full of hitches and hiccups, the last thing a leader's job involves is implementing the 'correct' recommendations. Because all the time you are running into situations for which no prescriptions exist to tell you what you can't or you mustn't do. Deadlock situations, for which there are no rules, to which foreign techniques do not apply, but which have to be resolved urgently, on an ad hoc basis. So that you feel the urge to say, 'Let's put it off, collect data and calculate the effect.' But what if the effect is incalculable? In that case conventional management thinking doesn't work, because it cannot cope with incalculable effects. And anyway you can't wait, because the situation will change while you are studying it.

There is only one thing for it: a readiness to adopt untried, non-standard decisions and – if I may utter a heresy – an ability to attune oneself to the system. This is hard to explain. In Russian the word 'system' has overtones of something heartless, lifeless, inhuman. In fact this isn't so. The economic system is a living thing, which as it grows absorbs human habits and norms, corrects itself as it goes and displays a character, will and stubbornness. The leader's task is not simply to see it as an object of control, but to be sensitive to it as a partner. Only then will your actions, if they are precisely calibrated, evoke a response from the system and, I would say, gain its goodwill. Then everything will work out. I mean, you know that according to Murphy's Law, the bread begins falling buttered side downward. But if at the right moment you exert your will and, despite everything, alter the trend and achieve a change of direction, people, falling under the spell of this willpower, will begin to act. And they will save the situation despite everything.

So, we should not copy from foreigners as a matter of course, nor paint beautiful pictures, nor offer dead recommendations, but in each case see the problem in an unbiased way, on the wing, and formulate a vision of the goal, how to reach it and how fast. And at the same time we should use this experience in order to perfect a new administrative style. That is what we mean when we proclaim the **Principle of the Priority of Management over Ideology.**

Someone once said that our world is good or bad to the extent that our decisions are good or bad. I believe this. We have little time or money. But we have a huge advantage over countries with conservative market traditions in our absence of stereotypes; and we will win out if we can take advantage of it. You will probably find it strange to hear this today. The forecasting mind displays inertia: when it is raining it seems as if it will never stop. But believe me, the future lies open before us, especially in today's world, which stands on the threshold of a new epoch. I don't want to utter trite phrases, but I think you have still to be convinced that what look like failings today will prove tomorrow to be the beginning of new trends in harmony with the needs of our time. Our country, which has experienced two drastic revolutions in a single century, is entering the new century itself renewed. However hard things are now, this is, believe me, an enormous advantage.

> 'Our world is good or bad to the extent that our decisions are good or bad.'

That is really all I wanted to say to you. My idea is simple and absolutely optimistic.

In olden days they used to say: **'When God sends trials he sends the strength to endure them.'** I think that, couched in different, more scientific terms, this could be made the most meaningful of our Parkinson's laws.

For ten years the liberal-conservatives have tried to fall in behind the successful countries of the departing century. It hasn't worked. This means that we need to operate on the level of the coming century.

For ten years a false choice has been imposed on the country between two conservative strategies, one right-conservative, the other left-retrogressive. But we of the centre reject them both because both are historically played out. No strategy for a breakthrough can be built on them.

> 'When God sends trials he sends the strength to endure them.'

This is a matter not of ideology but of survival, not of political games but of national salvation. Today Russia's territory, an eighth of the world's land area, is five times greater than its share of the world's population and, at a minimum, ten times greater than its share of world production. Unless this imbalance is rectified through an increase in national product and population, then sooner or later a correction will occur through a loss of territory. We already know how this happens. Recent world events have shorn us of all illusions.

So, let us not fall into the sin of despondency. It does not befit us, the descendants and heirs of a people who have more than once proved their ability to make a joint national effort, to lose faith in the future.

Russia's history holds many secrets of governance – when, in a seemingly hopeless situation, a number of well-aimed decisions break down the barrier between the people and the authorities. The last traces of mutual alienation dissolve in this phenomenal unity. All the Parkinson's laws we have spoken of begin to work, as it were, in reverse. The authorities become clever and effective, the people altruistic and self-sacrificing. And they pull the country through in spite of all gloomy prognostications and portents.

So the question is not whether we shall manage to endure our trials. The question is whether we are foredoomed to experience them. What is there to prevent us from building a system based on public trust in the authorities, a system in which the best qualities of the people are manifested not in extreme situations, but in an everyday, lasting way?

My answer is that there is nothing to prevent us.

And we will definitely do it. And we will do it with your help. Because we have simply no other option.

Diamandis's motto

The best way to predict the future is to create it yourself.

...from the Mayor's notepad

From the Mayor's notepad

Some laws collected and freely adapted by Yuri Luzhkov

Heller's Law
The first myth of management is that it exists.

The Mencken-Martin Classification
Those who can, do. Those who can't, teach. Those who cannot teach, administrate.

Spencer's Scale
A good manager can make a decision without enough facts, an outstanding manager with none.

Putt's Typology
All bosses fall into two categories: those who understand what they cannot manage and those who manage what they cannot understand.

Chisholm's Law
People will always understand instructions differently from the person who gives them.

Corollary
If you explain so clearly that nobody can misunderstand, somebody will.

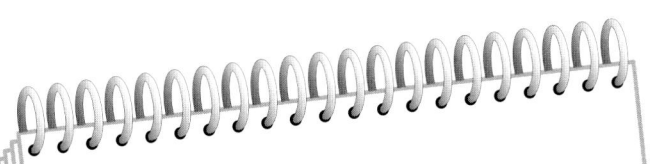

Luzhkov's Addendum
Profanity is the one language in which instructions will not be misunderstood.

Jacob's Law
To err is human – to blame it on someone else is even more human.

Kinkler's Law
Responsibility always exceeds authority.

Whistler's Axiom
You never know who is right, but you always know who is to blame.

Kettering's Principle
Logic is necessary in order to justify wrong decisions.

Corollary to Lord Falkland's Rule
Solving a known problem creates unknown ones.

Burke's Advice
Don't set a problem if you don't know the answer.

From the Chinese Book of Changes (I Ching)

If change is unnecessary, make no change.

Corollary

The more apparently insignificant a change the greater the unforeseen consequences.

The Persig-Luzhkov Postulate

The number of rational explanations is infinite. The number of rational actions is finite: as a rule, only one.

Howe's Observation

Everyone has a scheme that will not work.

The Snafu Lemma
Once you have exhausted all possibilities and fail, there will be one solution, simple and obvious, highly visible to everyone else.

Zymurgy's Law
People are always available for work in the past tense.

Dilbert's Law
Anyone can do any amount of work provided it isn't the work he/she is supposed to do.

Cornuelle's Law
Authority tends to assign jobs to those least able to do them.

Parkinson's Fourth Law
The number of people in any working group will increase regardless of the amount of work to be done.

Hendrickson's Law
If a problem causes many meetings, the meetings eventually become more important than the problem.

Old and Kahn's Theorem

The efficiency of a meeting is inversely proportional to the time spent and the number of participants.

Hlade's Law

If you have a difficult task, give it to a lazy person – they will find the easiest and quickest way to do it.

The Universal Work Input Paradox

The first 90% of a project takes 10% of the time, the last 10% takes the rest.

The Cheops-Resin Law*

Nothing ever gets built on schedule or within budget.

Golub's Extension

A carelessly planned project takes three times longer to complete than expected. A carefully planned project only takes twice as long.

Meskimen's Law

There's never time to do it right, but there's always time to do it over.

* Reference to Vladimir Resin (b 1936), first deputy mayor of Moscow responsible for building and planning issues.

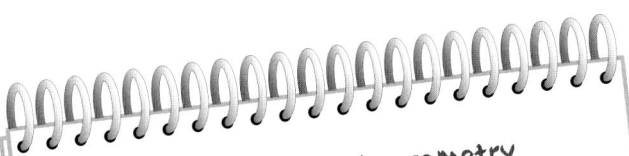

The Law of Applied Chaosometry
The more carefully a system is contrived, the greater the mess when something goes wrong.

Everitt's Law
When a country is in (forgive me) a bloody mess, only extremely hard work can counter that mess. Nevertheless, countering it will actually increase the overall mess.

The Russian Law of Probability
In Russia only the impossible happens.

Cooper's Postulate
New laws create new loopholes.

Free adaptation of Cooper's Postulate
New laws are created in order to create new loopholes.

The Russian way with the Law
If you mustn't but you need to, then you can.

Sausage Wisdom
People who love sausage and respect the law should never watch either one being made.

An allusion to The Tale of the Golden Fish with Boris Yeltsin as the fisherman.

Malek's Theorem
Any simple idea will be worded in the most complicated way.

Meyer's Equation
It is a simple task to make things complex, but a complex task to make them simple.

The Underling's First Commandment
Never let the boss see that you're cleverer than he is.

Ross's Advice

Never characterise the importance of a statement in advance.

> **WE'RE OUT OF MONEY, BUT WE'VE GOT ROUBLES**
>
> KACCA

Chisholm's Enigma

When you are sure everyone will like what you do, they are sure not to.

Horngren's Metapostulate

Among economists the real world is a special case.

Mars's Rule adapted by Luzhkov

An expert is anyone from the West.

Finagle's Law

Once a job is fouled up, anything done to improve it will make it worse.

Freeman's commentary on Ginsberg's Theorem

Before getting worse the situation will temporarily improve.

Another fairytale allusion, this time to a character in the prologue of Alexander Pushkin's Ruslan and Lyudmila, a 'learned cat' which is fettered to an oak tree by a golden chain. The cat, hanged by it's own chain, reflects the plight of Russia's nascent middle class.

Gattuso's Postulate

Nothing is ever so bad that it can't get worse.

Drazen's Law

The time it takes to rectify a situation is inversely proportional to the time it took to get worse.

Stockmayer's Indicator

If it looks easy it will be tough.

The Einstein-Ballance Theory of Relativity

How long a minute is depends on which side of the bathroom door you're on.

Jenning's Corollary to the Buttered Side Down Law

The chance of the bread falling with the buttered side down is directly proportional to the cost of the carpet.

Anthony's Law

Any tool when dropped will roll into the least accessible corner.

Simon's Law

Everything put together falls apart sooner or later.

> ONE WAY OR ANOTHER, WE SHALL GO FORWARD!
>
> COULDN'T WE TRY 'ANOTHER' RIGHT NOW

Segal's Paradox

A man with one watch knows what time it is - a man with two watches is never sure.

Miller's Theorem

You can't tell how deep a puddle is until you step in it.

Rune's Rule

If you don't care where you are, you ain't lost.